5-MINUTE
DEVOTIONS
FOR
GIRLS

A Tween's Weekly
Christian Devotional
for a Life of Hope,
Faith, and Love

MADE
EASY
PRESS

Producer & International Distributor
eBookPro Publishing
www.ebook-pro.com

5-MINUTE DEVOTIONS FOR GIRLS
A Tween's Weekly Devotional for a Life of Hope, Faith, and Love
Made Easy Press

Contact: agency@ebook-pro.com

ISBN 9798852493811

This book belongs to

....

Contents

Introduction

*"The Lord will watch over your coming and going
both now and forevermore."*

Psalms 121:8

Life can be busy, complicated, and sometimes even messy. It's easy to get caught up in school, activities, friends, homework, gossip, and drama, and sometimes we forget to hold onto what's really important. You are God's girl, and He loves you so much.

God's Word can lead you gently through life, guiding you and helping you understand who you are and what you can be.

This weekly journal, made especially for girls like you, will be your guide as you embark on a journey to connect with your faith.

It will encourage you to think and ask questions about yourself and the things you see around you, and in the end, it will bring you so much closer to our Heavenly Father, who is waiting for you with open arms.

How to Use This Book

"When they had read it, they rejoiced because of its encouragement."

Acts 15:31

This special book is divided into fifty-two weekly chapters to give you an entire year of devotions.

Once a week, take five minutes for yourself and open up where you left off. Each week begins with a Bible verse to read and be inspired by. The scripture is followed by a few words that will tell you more about what the particular Bible verse means, and how you may apply it to your life.

Next, pick up a pencil or pen and respond to the reflections that you are experiencing, that may be pressing on you, as you think, reminisce, and imagine.

At the end of every chapter, you'll find a weekly challenge – something to do that week that will strengthen your bond with God.

You can read these devotions alone or with a friend, a parent, or a sister. You could even do it with a whole group of friends! The important thing is to put aside some time every week, wherever and with whoever you want, and allow yourself to spend at least five minutes with the incredible Word of God.

FRIENDSHIP

"A friend loves at all times."

Proverbs 17:17

$\mathbf{A}$ good friend is one of the most valuable things you can have in your life. Some people have a lot of friends, and other people only have a few, or even just one.

The number of friends you have isn't important, what counts is who they are and how they affect your life.

How can you be a good friend?

The Bible tells us that being a good friend means "loving at all times."

Sometimes, it's hard for us to love our friends. There are days when we get upset or annoyed with them, or we just need some time to ourselves.

But to be a truly good friend, you must love and accept your friends for who they are every single day, even on hard days. And your friends should do the same for you!

Reflections

1. Who are your best friends?
   What do you appreciate most about them?

2. What kind of friend are you?

3. Do you have unconditional love for your friends?

4. Are there people in your life who are not true friends to you?

5. What can you do to improve your relationships with your friends?

6. Do you feel that God is a friend to you? In what way?

This week, make a one-on-one date with one of your friends. You can go for a walk, eat a meal together, or just sit and talk. Make sure you let them know how important and special they are to you.

Love Conquers All

"Above all, love each other deeply,
because love covers over a multitude of sins."

1 Peter 4:8

We Christians are commanded to work hard at loving one another.

We must love deeply, from our heart, not only our closest friends and family – but everyone we meet.

None of us is perfect. We all have flaws and have made mistakes, but when we truly love and are loved by others, we can forgive each other and overlook our imperfections.

So many wars and conflicts could have been avoided if people had spoken a language of love, not of hate.

Let's do our best to try and think of everyone and everything with love, and to work hard to perfect our love for our fellow Christians and for our Lord.

Reflections

1. Think about what love means to you. Which kinds of acts or words tell you that someone loves you?

2. What power does love hold?

3. Have you ever been in a situation where you felt that love helped you overcome hardship?

4. God loves you. How do you see this love in your life? What does He do for you?

5. How can you show your love for God better?

This week, tell someone that you love them every day.

PURPOSE

"And we know that in all things God works for the good of those who love Him, who have been called according to His purpose."

Romans 8:28

In this week's special Bible passage, we learn that God is in control of all things, and He "works for the good of those who love Him." What does this tell us?

We are God's children, and we have been called according to his purpose. And when we fulfill our purpose, which is to be good and faithful and to believe in the Lord, He looks out for us and makes good things happen in our lives.

It is sometimes hard to know what your own personal purpose is. What you can be sure of is that God knows exactly what your purpose is on this Earth, and He will shepherd you there.

You may never know exactly what purpose He destines for you, and that's ok!

If you lead a light-filled life under the grace of God, you can trust that you are fulfilling your purpose.

Reflections

1. We all have a purpose in our life. What do you think your purpose is in this world?

2. What is God's purpose for you?

3. Sometimes, we lose sight of our purpose. How can we work to remember it?

4. How does God "call" to you?

5. Have you heard His voice?

This week, listen for God's voice as you live your life. It can be anywhere and at any time.

EMPATHY

"Be happy with those who are happy, and cry with those who are crying."

Romans 12:15

Have you ever seen someone who was sad and it made you feel sad yourself?

Or has anyone in your life ever been so happy that just seeing them filled you with joy?

That feeling, when you put yourself in someone else's shoes and feel what they're feeling, is called empathy.

Empathy is a powerful thing. It lets us share in others' experiences and brings us closer together. God commands us to have empathy for others because that is how we build friendships, connections, and community. Having empathy also makes you a better friend, because when you feel someone else's feelings as your own, it's easier to understand their troubles and triumphs and to recognize when they need help.

You can be more empathetic by practicing putting yourself in someone else's shoes and thinking about what you would feel like in their situation. Sharing your own feelings with your friends and family is also good empathy practice!

Reflections

1. What makes you sad?

2. What makes you happy?

3. When has someone shown you empathy? How?

4. When have you shown a friend empathy?

5. Can you show empathy for someone you don't know? How?

This week, be extra aware of how your friends are feeling. Talk to them and try to help when they're down, and celebrate with them when they're happy.

Forgiveness

*"Be kind and compassionate to one another,
forgiving each other, just as in Christ God forgave you."*

Ephesians 4:32

The power to forgive is a very important virtue.
You might ask, why? If someone does something to me that's mean or hurtful, why should I forgive them?

When someone chooses to act in a way that is bad or wrong, like calling you names, gossiping about you, or hurting you in any other way, that is their choice.

But their choice has nothing to do with you! God will judge them for how they act, but it is up to you to decide how you react to what they do.

Forgiveness brings peace.

When you find it in you to forgive that person who did you wrong, you are saying, "I will not let someone else control me." You are letting yourself move on and be the bigger person.

When you truly forgive with all your heart, you are doing God's work and He will reward you for it!

Reflections

1. Why is it sometimes hard to forgive?

....

....

2. Think of a time when someone hurt you.

....

....

3. Have you forgiven them?

....

....

4. If not, what do you think you need to do to forgive them?

....

....

5. Why is it so important to forgive others?

....

....

....

....

....

This week, make an effort to forgive someone who hurt you. It could be for something that just happened or for something that happened a while ago. You don't have to tell them, but make an effort to fully forgive them in your heart.

SELF-CONTROL

*"Be not quick in your spirit to become angry,
for anger lodges in the heart of fools."*

Ecclesiastes 7:9

What is something that makes you really mad?

Getting mad is a natural reaction. It's okay to be mad now and then, but it's also important to practice controlling your anger.

The Bible says that people who are quick to get angry and slow to forgive are fools. Why is that?

It's because being mad doesn't actually help the situation, and it probably won't make you feel better, either.

When you start to feel angry about something, there are a few things you can do to calm down.

You can close your eyes and take deep, deep breaths.

You can talk to someone about why you're mad. Sometimes just talking helps!

You can take yourself away from the situation until you feel better.

And you can lean on God and your connection with Him to bring peace to your heart.

Reflections

1. Do you get angry often? Who do you get most angry with?

....

....

2. Draw a picture of what your anger feels like.

3. Think of a time when you were really mad.
   Did being mad make you feel better or worse

....

....

4. What do you do to stay calm when you feel angry?

....

....

5. Do you know anyone who never ever gets mad?
   How do you think they do it?

....

....

This week, practice being calm by doing deep breathing exercises twice a day. Every morning and every evening, spend two minutes just breathing in and out with your eyes closed.

YOU ARE NEVER ALONE

"Be strong and courageous. Do not fear or be in dread of them, for it is the Lord your God who goes with you. He will not leave you or forsake you."

Deuteronomy 31:6

Do you ever feel alone?

Sometimes we can feel lonely even when we are surrounded by people. Loneliness has to do with how we feel on the inside, not on the outside.

Close your eyes and try to imagine that God is there with you. Do you feel Him?

Our heavenly Father isn't up in the sky, or far away somewhere that we can't reach Him. He lives within every single one of us, and within you as well.

He's there, just waiting for you to reach out and take His hand.

How can you ever be alone when He is always there with you?

"He will not leave you or forsake you." Trust that He is by your side and goes with you wherever you go.

Reflections

1. Think of a time when you were all alone. How did you feel?

2. Do you feel the presence of God even when you are by yourself?

3. Make a list of three things that make you feel better when you're lonely.

4. How can your closeness with God help you feel less alone?

5. Write down these words: "I am never alone."

This week, whatever you do, try to feel God with you. At home, at school, or at church, open your heart to feel Him close.

ANXIETY

*"Cast all your anxieties on Him,
because He cares for you."*

1 Peter 5:7

Anxiety is the feeling of being overwhelmed, of being worried, or uneasy, in a way that disturbs your peace.

You might be anxious about a test you have coming up, about a big presentation you have to make, a show you're performing in, or anything else that feels like a lot to deal with.

Your strong, unwavering faith in God can help you get past these anxieties. God is always looking out for you, and He wants what's best for you.

When you feel anxious or overwhelmed, take a deep breath and try to speak to God. Share with Him how you feel, and trust in Him and in yourself that you can get past whatever it is that you're afraid of.

"Cast all your anxieties on Him", the Bible says. It's important to know that you can share your anxieties with Heavenly Father, and seek His guidance. That's exactly what faith is about – having a relationship with God and letting Him into your life.

Reflections

1. Have you ever felt anxious or nervous?

2. What makes you feel that way?

3. Who helps you calm yourself when you're anxious?

4. What do you think "casting your anxieties on God" means?

5. Do you think that if you "cast your anxieties" on God, it can help?

This week, whenever you feel anxious, take a deep breath and remember that He is always there, looking out for you. Remind yourself that everything will be okay.

REST

"Come to me, all you who are weary and burdened,
and I will give you rest."

Matthew 11:28

Do you know that everyone in the world needs to rest?

Even God Himself, after completing His wonderful creation in six astonishing days, rested on the seventh day.

Resting and taking time for yourself is an important way of taking care of yourself. What makes you feel rested after a long day?

It could be reading a book, doing some arts or crafts, writing in your journal, saying your prayers, or just spending some time with your family.

God is there with you, always, reminding you to come to Him when you are weary or burdened. Many people find rest and calm in worshipping Him, and I encourage you to try praying, reading scripture, or simply talking to God the next time you feel overwhelmed.

It can work wonders!

Reflections

1. What are your favorite things to do in your free time?

2. What makes you feel rested?

3. Do you think that God can have a part in your life outside of church?

4. Where?

5. How can you incorporate your faith into your hobbies?

This week, take time to allow God a place in your times of rest. You can speak to Him before bed, write to Him, or add a daily prayer to your routine.

PERSEVERANCE

*"Consider it pure joy, my brothers and sisters,
whenever you face trials of many kinds,
because you know that the testing of your faith
produces perseverance."*

James 1:2-3

We all face "trials" in life. A trial can be having difficulty with a subject at school, not getting accepted onto the sports or cheerleading team you were hoping for, or arguing with your parents. It can even be as simple as having a hard day or getting a not-so-great grade on a test.

But our kind and loving Father loves you and wants what is best for you – and even if you can't see it, each and every trial He puts in your path is a lesson for you to learn and grow from.

One of the lessons that hardship teaches us is the lesson of perseverance, or in other words, not giving up.

When you face a trial, it is God's way of telling you, lovingly, how much He believes in you and in your power to persevere. He is helping you to see just how strong and courageous you can be, and every time you overcome a trial, He helps you grow into a more capable, amazing young woman.

Reflections

1. What kinds of "trials" do you face?

2. Everyone wants to give up sometimes. Have you ever given up on something because it was too hard?

3. What does the Bible mean when it says that something "tests your faith"?

4. What does it mean to persevere?

5. Are you good at persevering, or could you be better?

6. How can we find joy in difficulty?

This week, do something you've been avoiding because it feels hard. Persevere, and don't be afraid of a challenge!

Week 11

HUMILITY

"Do nothing from selfish ambition or conceit, but in humility count others more significant than yourselves. Let each of you look not only to his own interests, but also to the interests of others."

Philippians 2:3-4

Being humble is exactly the opposite of being prideful. Someone who is prideful thinks that they are better than others and that their wants and needs are more important.

Kids at school who are prideful might not let other kids play with them, or they might be condescending towards them.

But humility means thinking about others more than you think about yourself. It is about doing good deeds because that is what's right, without expecting praise or reward.

The key to being humble is understanding that everyone – you, your family, your friends, and perfect strangers – are God's amazing creations, and are all created equal. God loves us all as His children and He expects and wants us to love and be good to one another.

Humility is one of the words that best describe the life of Christ – and he should be a role model to us all.

Reflections

1. Think of a time when you were selfish.

2. Now, think of a time when you behaved in a humble way.

3. When did you feel better – after you were selfish, or after you were humble?

4. How can you take an interest in what other people like?

5. List something special about three different people in your life.

This week, practice humility by taking an interest in your friends and family and putting others before you.

JUDGMENT

"Don't judge according to appearances.
Judge with right judgment."

John 7:24

Some people look very different from us. They can have different hair or skin color, wear different clothes, eat different food, or like different things. But deep down inside, the same heart beats in them as it does in us.

It is not our job to judge other people by how they look and behave.

But it is important to know the difference between good and bad – that is what's called "right judgment."

To judge rightly, we need to know God and put our faith in Him. Then, we can be sure that the way we judge people is based on truth, and not on our own thoughts and opinions.

Have you ever thought badly about someone just because of how they looked, where they lived, or what they wore? True strength lies in accepting other people and loving them for who they are.

Reflections

1. Have you ever judged someone before you knew them?

....

....

2. What should you judge other people by, if not by their appearance?

....

....

3. What do you think "right judgment" means?

....

....

4. Do you think that God judges you?

....

....

5. If He does, what part of you does He judge? How you look or how you act?

....

....

....

....

This week, be aware of how you judge people. Be kind and fair in your thoughts, and try to see the light in every single person.

Temptation

"No temptation has overtaken you that is not common to man. God is faithful, and He will not let you be tempted beyond your ability, but with the temptation He will also provide the way of escape, that you may be able to endure it."

1 Corinthians 10:13

Your world is full of temptations.

Screen time can be a temptation, or eating too much candy, or playing with your friends even though you should be doing your homework.

The Bible tells us that if we trust in God, He will not let us be tempted so much that we can't resist the temptation. It also says that "with the temptation, He will also provide the way of escape".

How can you escape temptation?

Even if you don't know it, your spirit is stronger than you think. You know the difference between right and wrong, because you are smart and faithful. So as soon as you're tempted by something that is wrong or bad, you can draw on your connection with God and the help of your family and friends to resist that temptation and find the right path.

God always gives you a way to escape temptation. But it is up to you to take the path that He shows you and always choose to do what is right, and not what is wrong.

Reflections

1. What are things that tempt you?

2. Is temptation always a bad thing?

3. Do you feel good or bad after giving in to temptation?

4. How can the love of God save you from temptation?

5. What can you do the next time you are tempted by something that is wrong?

This week, choose one temptation you'd like to resist. Remember to persist!

The Future

"For I know the plans I have for you,
declares the Lord, plans for welfare and not for evil,
to give you a future and a hope."

Jeremiah 29:11

I promise you that the Lord has so much in store for you. He knows what you'll do, where you'll live, and what you will accomplish. And his plans for you are full of good, happy things.

But sometimes, He chooses not to share those things with you.

Why is that?

Imagine watching a movie, or reading a book. Just before you start the first page, someone tells you what happens in the end. Isn't that annoying? And doesn't it make you not want to watch the movie or read the book anymore?

If we knew all that God had in store for us, we might not feel the need to work hard, be good, and overcome the challenges that life brings us.

Not knowing everything that will happen to us leaves us room for hopefulness and aspiration – and it makes life so much more interesting, surprising, and exciting!

Reflections

1. Do you think that God has a plan for you and for everyone else in your life?

2. Are there things that you want in your future?

3. Do you believe you can ask God to steer your life onto a certain path?

4. When have you felt that things in your life haven't happened how you expected?

5. Looking back, do you think that was part of God's plan for you?

This week, be mindful of how things turn out. Remember that even if things don't go according to your plan, God's plan for you is always in play.

Be a Positive Force

"Therefore encourage one another and build each other up, just as in fact you are doing."

1 Thessalonians 5:11

The Bible tells us to "encourage" one another and "build" each other up.

Some people in our world are a positive force in our lives, and other people can be a negative force. Your parents who love and keep you safe are a positive force, and a teacher or mentor who helps you learn and grow is a positive force. A good friend who accepts you as you are is a positive force, as well.

People who are negative forces don't encourage you and can sometimes even put you down. Can you think of anyone who has that kind of effect on your life?

Now, think about what you are for other people. Are you a positive, encouraging force in your parents', siblings', and friends' lives? Do you lift them up, help them when they're down, and encourage them to be better?

You have the power and the ability to be a positive force in so many people's lives.

Reflections

1. Who is a positive force in your life?

   ....

   ....

   ....

2. Why is it so important to be a positive force in other people's lives?

   ....

   ....

   ....

3. How can you "build someone up" instead of putting them down?

   ....

   ....

   ....

4. What are some good words of encouragement you can use?

   ....

   ....

   ....

   ....

   ....

This week, write some words of encouragement to a friend or family member who needs them.

GRATITUDE

"Give thanks to the Lord, for He is good;
His love endures forever."

Psalms 107:1

You have so much in your life to be grateful for!

You have people who care about you and keep you safe, clothes to wear, food to eat, a home and a bed to sleep in, your health, your talents, and your education.

Sometimes, we take the things we have for granted. It's a very natural thing, and we all do it, even if we don't mean to.

Take a minute, now, to reflect on all of the things you have and are thankful for.

Who gave you all of these things?

Everything you have is bestowed upon you by the goodness of God. He puts kind and generous people in your life to watch over you and do His work, and you must remember always to be thankful for Him and for all He has given you.

"His love endures forever" – and for that, we are eternally grateful.

Reflections

1. List five things you are thankful for, right now.

2. How can we show our gratitude to the people we love who take care of us?

3. How can we show our gratitude to the Lord?

4. What do you think it means that "His love endures forever"?

This week, express your gratitude. Every evening, write down three things you're thankful for today.

CHARITY

"Each of you should give what you have decided in your heart to give, not reluctantly or under compulsion, for God loves a cheerful giver. And God is able to bless you abundantly, so that in all things at all times, having all that you need, you will abound in every good work."

2 Corinthians 9:6-8

You are so fortunate that you have so many good things in your life, and people who love you.

But remember, there are people everywhere who are less fortunate than you!

Some kids don't have enough food to eat three meals a day, or clean clothes to wear. As Christians, it is our duty and our privilege to be able to help others in need.

When you give to others, you should do it cheerfully, from the goodness of your heart. People who have less than you do are still people, who deserve to be treated with compassion and respect.

So, when you choose to give your time, money, or possessions to charity, do it with happiness in your heart, knowing that what you are doing makes the Lord proud that you are taking care of His children.

Reflections

1. Is there anyone in your life who is less fortunate than you?

2. What does "charity" mean to you?

3. What can we learn from the stories of the Bible about being charitable?

4. How can we, as good Christians, help others who are in need?

This week, do an act of charity. You can donate old clothes or toys that are in good condition, help someone in need, or volunteer.

HONESTY

*"I know, my God, that you test the heart
and are pleased with integrity."*

1 Chronicles 29:17

Being honest with the people in your life means choosing to tell them the truth and not deceiving them.

Sometimes, we want to tell lies and we convince ourselves that they are only white lies, and they won't hurt anyone.

But lies are a funny thing – they like company. Once you start being dishonest, it's difficult to stop. And the more dishonest you are with other people, the more dishonest you will begin to be with yourself.

How can you be dishonest with yourself, you might ask?

You may say to yourself, "I'm only borrowing this pen from a friend without asking, I'll give it back." But deep down, you know that stealing is wrong.

God expects us to live a life of truth and integrity, and only then can we be complete in our faith.

Reflections

1. Think about a time when you were dishonest. How did you feel after telling a lie?

2. Why is God pleased with integrity?

3. Why is it so important to be honest with yourself?

4. Do you think that God knows when you are dishonest?

This week, be truly honest with yourself and the people around you. Reflect on what you do and how you feel, and think twice before speaking dishonestly, even if it's just a little white lie.

Seeing the Good

*"God promises to make something good out of the
storms that bring devastation to your life."*

Romans 8:28

Everyone has good days and bad days.

Sometimes, things happen that seem bad – like if someone insults you, or you lose or break something, or someone you love passes away.

God promises us that even things that look like "storms" in life, hide some good in them.

When Joseph was thrown into the pit by his brothers, he was sad and thought that his life was ruined, but he was rescued from that hole and ended up as Pharaoh's right-hand man!

Lots of stories in the Bible teach us that we should see the good even in the very worst things that happen to us.

When you feel disappointed or sad, sit and reflect on what good might possibly come from the bad. Focusing on the good in everything will make you a happier, more positive person. It also shows that you have complete trust in the Lord that He has amazing plans for you, even if you don't know what they are yet!

Reflections

1. What kinds of things in your life feel like a "storm"?

2. How can you keep these "storms" from breaking you?

3. Have you ever had something bad happen to you, but then realized there was good in it after all?

4. Why do you think that God allows bad things to happen sometimes?

5. What can challenges teach us?

This week, at the end of every day, look back and think of something bad or annoying that happened to you. Write it down, then next to it write down something good that might come of the bad.

TRUST

"Trust in the Lord with all your heart, and do not lean on your own understanding. In all your ways acknowledge Him, and He will make straight your paths."

Proverbs 3:5-6

One of the most important core values of Christianity is *trust*.

We trust all kinds of different people in our life.

You trust your parents to do what's best for you and help you grow.

You trust your teachers to give you a good education.

You trust doctors to take care of you and make you better when you're sick.

But most important of all is the trust that you have in God. When you truly put your trust in Him and acknowledge His greatness, there is nothing you can't do.

So, we trust that He is our creator, that He loves us, has a plan for us, and never leaves us alone.

And, in return, He showers us with happiness and comfort.

Reflections

1. How can you acknowledge the Lord every single day?

2. When have you felt that your path wasn't straight?

3. How did you get back onto a straight path?

4. What does it mean to "trust in the Lord with all your heart"?

This week, make a habit of acknowledging the Lord every single day, however feels right to you.

COURAGE

"Have I not commanded you? Be strong and courageous.
Do not be frightened, and do not be dismayed,
for the Lord your God is with you wherever you go."

Joshua 1:9

Why is it important for the Bible to tell us to be courageous?

Your faith in God is based on complete trust and the knowledge that He is by your side, guiding you every day and keeping you protected.

If that is the case, then what do you have to fear?

Courage is not something that you either have or don't have. Anyone and everyone can learn to be courageous, and so can you.

So when you feel scared about doing something that you know is right, like standing up for yourself or others, know that by being strong and courageous, you are doing God's command.

And He will reward you for your strength and loyalty to Him.

Reflections

1. Think about a time when you didn't feel courageous.

   ....

   ....

2. Now, think of a time when you did.

   ....

   ....

3. Who is the most courageous person in your life?

   ....

   ....

   ....

4. What does it mean to have courage?

   ....

   ....

   ....

5. How can God help you find your courage when you're afraid?

   ....

   ....

   ....

This week, do something that makes you scared. Remember to be strong and courageous, but don't do anything dangerous!

Taking Action

*"Dear children, let us not love with words or speech
but with actions and in truth."*

1 John 3:18

When your parents kiss you good night, they probably tell you "I love you" and you say it back to them.

It's important to tell the people in your life that you love them. But it's even more important to *show* them.

"Actions speak louder than words" – and they mean more. When someone looks after you when you're sick, does something to make you happy, or gives you a gift, and they do it from the bottom of their heart, they are showing you with their actions how much you mean to them.

When we worship God every day, we need to do more than just use our words. Praying is important, yes, but using your actions to prove your devotion means so much more!

When you take the time to go to Church on Sunday or on holidays, when you are kind and good to others, when you are modest and humble, all of these things are ways to show God your love.

Reflections

1. Who are the people you love the most?

_____

_____

_____

2. How often do you tell these people that you love them?

_____

_____

_____

3. How can you show that you love them?

_____

_____

_____

4. How can you _show_ God the love you have for Him?

_____

_____

_____

This week, use your actions, not only your words, to show God and the people in your life just how much you love them.

BELIEVE IN YOURSELF

"I can do all this through Him who gives me strength."

Philippians 4:13

In this special verse from the Bible, Paul tells us that with God's help, we can do anything we've ever dreamed of.

Our Heavenly Father fills us with strength every day, through prayer, love, and worship. When you walk a path of light and faithfulness, He rewards you with the power to fulfill all of your dreams.

When you look in the mirror and say to yourself, "I believe in you!", you are trusting that God will give you strength. You are acknowledging that everything you can do is thanks to Him, and that He is great and benevolent.

So the next time you're not sure you can do something, open your heart to God and believe that He will help you achieve it.

Reflections

1. How does God give you strength?

....

....

2. What does it mean to believe in yourself?

....

....

3. Who else believes in you?

....

....

4. Do you ever have trouble believing in yourself?

....

....

5. When?

....

....

....

....

This week, stand in front of the mirror every day and give yourself a compliment. Believe in yourself!

HOSPITALITY

"So welcome each other, in the same way that Christ also welcomed you, for God's glory."

Romans 15:7

In the book of Genesis, Abraham welcomed weary travelers into his tent on a hot day. He gave them his food and drink, and offered them a place to rest, even though he didn't have much himself.

In return, Abraham was rewarded for his hospitality with a son, Isaac.

Abraham's willingness to give what is his to people who were complete strangers can teach us a lot about hospitality.

Being hospitable means welcoming others into your home and your life and sharing with them what you have.

When you invite a friend over, you can show hospitality by offering them a drink or a snack, sharing your toys and games with them, and even letting them sit in the comfortable chair or play a video game first.

Reflections

1. Do you have a home that welcomes others?

2. How can you make your home a more welcoming place?

3. How can you make your heart more welcoming toward other people?

4. Do you feel welcomed by Christ?

5. How? And where?

This week, welcome someone into your home or your room. Make sure they are comfortable and practice the skill of hospitality.

IMMORTALITY

*"Jesus said to her, 'I am the resurrection and the life.
The one who believes in me will live, even though they die;
and whoever lives by believing in me will never die.'"*

John 11:25-26

Jesus says to us, "whoever lives by believing in me will never die."

Let's break down what this means.

No one is immortal. Our bodies grow old and eventually, we pass away. But what about our souls, the true essence of us that does not need a body to live?

We each have a soul.

Your soul is what makes you *you*, what makes you special and different from other people. When you trust in God and worship Him, your soul gets stronger and shines brighter than ever.

If you believe in Jesus Christ faithfully for all your life, then your soul will live on forever, spreading light and hope throughout the world.

Reflections

1. What do you think "resurrection" means?

....

....

....

2. What did Jesus mean when he said, "whoever lives by believing in me will never die"?

....

....

....

3. How can we keep living even when we die?

....

....

....

4. What good can we do to make a better world in God's name?

....

....

....

....

....

This week, talk to someone you love about their faith, and ask them how they think that believing in God makes them immortal.

Good and Bad

"Let love be genuine. Abhor what is evil;
hold fast to what is good."

Romans 12:9

Knowing good from bad and right from wrong is something we're taught from when we're little kids. At a young age, children don't always know what is ok and what is not.

But when you're older, and already starting to grow up and becoming a young woman, it's very important that you know the difference between what is good and what is bad.

God put you on this earth and gave you brains, talents, and an incredible life! In return, He asks that you "abhor what is evil."

Deep in your heart, you know the difference between good and bad. "Bad" can sometimes be tempting, like doing something you want to do even though your parents told you not to do it.

Deep down, you know that they are right and they want what is best for you.

That is why you have to dig deep and be strong enough to always stick to the good. That is what God wants from you – and that is what will bring you closer to Him.

Reflections

1. What are some good values?

2. What are some bad values?

3. How can we tell the difference between something that is "good" and something that is "bad"?

4. Think of a time when you saw someone doing something that you knew was bad. How did you react?

5. How would you react now if it happened again?

This week, write down every time you see someone perform an act of good.

Waking Up

*"Let the morning bring me word of Your unfailing love,
for I have put my trust in You. Show me the way I should go,
for to You I entrust my life."*

Psalms 143:8

Every morning, you wake up, stretch your arms, and get out of bed.

Have you ever stopped to think about how wonderful it is that you get to wake up every day and start fresh?

God gave you incredible skin, muscles, a brain, and a heart, and they all work together to keep you alive and healthy every day.

When you get up and get ready for the day, remember who made that possible.

Take time in the morning to talk to God, even just to thank Him for watching over you in the night and making sure your dreams were sweet.

Reflections

1. What is the first thing you do every morning?

2. What is your favorite thing about waking up to a new day?

3. How can you change your morning routine to allow
   your faith to be a bigger part of it?

4. How does God "show you the way you should go"?

This week, every morning when you wake up, say a prayer.
Make God the first thought of your day.

Purity

"Blessed are the pure in heart, for they shall see God."

Matthew 5:8

A pure heart shows in how you think, how you speak, which words you use, the choices you make, what you wear, and how you behave.

When you make sure to keep your heart and thoughts pure, your soul is at peace and can be closer to God. Remember that living in purity not only helps you, but all the people around you as well.

But how to stay pure?

The Bible tells us to be "pure in heart". Being pure in your heart means never thinking badly of anyone else, banishing jealous thoughts, and keeping God in your mind at all times. It's not enough to only behave nicely to others, you need to truly think well of them in your head.

Everyone sins sometimes, and that's ok. If you ever have thoughts that you feel are impure, the best thing to do is to have a conversation with God. Confess to Him about your thoughts, and let Him help guide you back to the right path.

Just talking about something can take a weight off your shoulders and help you do better next time!

Reflections

1. What does it mean to be "pure"?

2. What is the difference between being physically pure and having pure thoughts?

3. What helps you stay pure?

4. Is there anything you have a guilty conscience about?

5. What can you do to clear your guilty conscience?

This week, focus on keeping your heart and thoughts pure and clean.

SUCCESS

*"May He give you the desire of your heart
and make all your plans succeed."*

Psalms 20:4

Being "successful" can mean lots of different things.

People who are famous and have lots of money can be considered successful. But even people who have little money and are not famous for anything can be just as successful.

A mom or dad who does a good job is a successful parent. A teacher who is kind, smart, and considerate is a successful teacher. Someone who gets good grades at school is a successful student.

Success means achieving the goals that you set for yourself.

If your goal is to get a good grade on a test and you manage, that's a success! If you want to score a goal in your soccer game and you do, that's success too. If you want to help your parents out around the house and you do some more chores that save them time, that's another success.

When you pray to God and welcome Him into your life, He will help all your dreams and desires come true.

Reflections

1. What does it mean to be successful?

   ....

   ....

2. Who is the most successful person you know? Why?

   ....

   ....

3. What plans do you have for your life?

   ....

   ....

4. Do you think you need to work for your success,
   or will God take care of everything for you?

   ....

   ....

5. How can you help God steer your life to success?

   ....

   ....

   ....

   ....

This week, make a list of the things you would like to accomplish in your life.

HOPE

*"May the God of hope fill you with all joy and peace
as you trust in Him, so that you may overflow
with hope by the power of the Holy Spirit."*

Romans 15:13

Having faith goes together with having hope.

When you truly have faith in the Lord and in His power to do anything, you can be confident that He will provide you with a good and happy future.

Hope means being optimistic, and looking forward to the future.

It means knowing that life can always get better and that good things are waiting.

Hope can help you through hard times by imagining what will be and putting your trust in God to do what He can for your happiness.

When your heart is full of hope, you are telling God that you love and trust Him always!

Reflections

1. Why is hope so important?

2. What makes you feel hopeful?

3. What do you hope for the people you love?

4. What do you hope for yourself?

5. What do you hope for your future?

This week, think about things that make you angry or sad. Let your heart fill with hope for how things can and will be better in the future.

FREEDOM

*"Now the Lord is the Spirit, and where the
Spirit of the Lord is, there is freedom."*

2 Corinthians 3:17

Freedom can mean something else to you than it does for someone else.

Freedom can be the summer vacation, or running outside in the yard, or finishing your homework early, or getting to pick out which clothes you want to wear in the morning.

Sometimes, we don't feel free – like when we have to go to school or do our chores. But there is a type of freedom that is *inside* you. When you follow the Spirit of the Lord, that freedom inside you will never stop!

The Lord's Spirit can set your heart and soul free and let you see the truth – that faith in God is the ultimate freedom.

Reflections

1. When do you feel free?

....
....
....

2. What does "freedom" mean to you?

....
....
....

3. Where do you feel the Spirit of the Lord in your life?

....
....
....

4. How can the Spirit of the Lord give you freedom?

....
....
....
....
....
....

This week, dig deep and find the things that make you feel truly free.

COMMUNITY

"Once you were not a people,
but now you are the people of God;
once you had not received mercy,
but now you have received mercy."

1 Peter 2:10

What does it mean to "be a people"?

You are always a part of something bigger. A part of your family, a part of your class at school, a part of your neighborhood, a part of your church, a part of your country even. You are even a small part of all the Christians in the world!

Being part of something bigger means having a community.

A community is a group of people who look out for you and are kind of like another family.

Communities come together to help each other out and to raise money when someone is sick or in need. When you are part of a community, it's your responsibility to help out too – so that when you need help, someone else can help you.

Reflections

1. Which communities do you have in your life? It could be your family, friends, neighborhood, Church, sports team, or any other group.

2. Why is it important to belong to a community?

3. How is being a part of a community better than being alone?

4. What can you do to benefit your community?

5. Do you feel a part of the community of all the people of God? How?

This week, do something good for your community and reflect on how grateful you are to have them by your side.

BEAUTY

"One thing I ask from the Lord, this only do I seek:
that I may dwell in the house of the Lord
all the days of my life, to gaze on the beauty of the Lord
and to seek Him in His temple."

Psalms 27:4

Our world is beautiful and amazing, filled with God's wondrous creations.

From huge oceans and sprawling deserts to the tiniest flowers and littlest bugs, each and every thing is unique and created with a purpose.

The beauty that we see all around us is proof of God's incredible power and His care.

When you walk around outside and take in the fresh air, trees, flowers, and animals, pay attention to how complicated and intricate everything is. Even you yourself – everything from your hair and your eyes to your freckles and fingernails serves a purpose, and is a part of what makes you you.

Reflections

1. How does the beauty of the Lord come across through His creations in our world?

2. What do you think is the most beautiful thing in the world?

3. What is the difference between outer and inner beauty?

4. Which do you think is more important?

5. How can you work on your inner beauty?

This week, take a long walk through nature to appreciate the beauty of God's creation.

COMFORT

"Praise be to the God and Father of our Lord Jesus Christ, the Father of compassion and the God of all comfort, who comforts us in all our troubles, so that we can comfort those in any trouble with the comfort we ourselves receive from God."

2 Corinthians 1:3-4

There are people and places in your life that bring you comfort. Maybe it's your room, one of your siblings, the library, a cousin, even a beloved pet.

These people and places make you feel better when you're down or cheer you up when you are sad.

As Christians, we are lucky to also have God to turn to for comfort.

He is always there, and always waiting for us to come and seek comfort in His arms.

If you ever feel upset, mad, or just not so happy, you can always turn to your faith and prayer to find the comfort that God has to give each and every one of us. He will never turn you away!

Reflections

1. When do you feel most comfortable?

2. Who comforts you in times of trouble?

3. How can you comfort others in their own times of trouble?

4. Write about a time when you gave comfort to someone else.

5. How can you find comfort in your faith?

This week, be aware of the people around you and how they are feeling. Try to provide comfort to someone who needs it.

CHILDREN OF GOD

*"See what great love the Father has lavished on us,
that we should be called children of God!"*

1 John 3:1

Heavenly Father treats His believers exactly as if they were His children.

Not everyone can be a child of God!

Those who believe in the Lord our Savior with all their heart and are faithful to him, God will take care of and love, like a father loves his child.

You are a beloved daughter of God, and so are all the other good Christians you have in your life. We are like one big happy family, and God is our shepherd.

Reflections

1. What does it mean to be a "child of God"?

2. Who do you think are children of God?

3. Do you ever feel like a child of God?

4. How is God like a father to you?

This week, bask in the love you feel from God.

WISDOM

"So be careful to live your life wisely, not foolishly."

Ephesians 5:15

Has anyone you know ever been described as wise?

Wisdom is different from knowledge. You can learn a lot of things at school and read lots of books and you will be very knowledgeable.

But wisdom is the ability to make good decisions, to use your experience and smarts to judge if something is good or bad, and to be able to teach other people the things you know.

God asks us to behave wisely, not foolishly.

In this, He means to tell us that we should think before we act and use the knowledge we have to make good choices that benefit us and our surroundings.

The Bible teaches us wisdom with its stories and lessons, and we can learn wisdom from people in our life that we admire – like parents, grandparents, teachers, even friends.

Reflections

1. What is the difference between being smart and being wise?

2. Who is the wisest person you know?

3. Do you ever behave foolishly, instead of wisely?

4. Think of an example of a time when you acted foolishly.

5. What could you have done in that situation that would have been wiser?

This week, when you make decisions, compare your choices and decide which ones are foolish and which are wise. Do your best to make only wise choices.

MATERIAL THINGS

"So do not worry, saying, 'What shall we eat?'
or 'What shall we drink?' or "What shall we wear?'
For the pagans run after all these things,
and your heavenly Father knows that you need them.
But seek first His kingdom and His righteousness,
and all these things will be given to you as well."

Matthew 6:31-34

There are two different kinds of things in this world – material things and immaterial things. Material things are ones that you can see and touch. Things like food, clothing, games, electronics, and books.

Immaterial things are things that you can feel and sense but don't have a physical shape. Things like love, trust, fear, faith, happiness, courage, and God.

We need both kinds of things to live a happy life. We need food to nourish us, clothes to wear, and things to bring us joy. But we need to be careful not to chase after material things too much, and to remember where true meaning lies – in our faith and loyalty to the Lord.

It's okay to enjoy things in life. We even use material things, like churches, wine, and prayer books to guide us and help us practice our faith.

Just so long as you always remember that material things come and go, but your faith in the Lord is forever.

Reflections

1. Why do we need material things like food, clothing, and electronics?

....

....

....

2. Do you ever feel that you are too attached to material things?

....

....

....

3. How can you be less dependent on these things?

....

....

....

4. What are some immaterial things that are important in life?

....

....

....

....

....

This week, try to take a step back from the material and focus more on spiritual things like love, faith, kindness, and goodness.

EVERYTHING IS POSSIBLE

"Jesus looked at them and said,
'With man this is impossible, but not with God;
all things are possible with God.'"

Mark 10:27

Jesus says that there are some things that are impossible for "man," or for human beings, to do alone.

Then, He says that with God – all things are possible.

Have you ever felt that something was impossible?

Think about all the wonderful things God has done. The world He has created, the flowers and trees He has grown, the huge oceans He has formed, and the creatures He has put on Earth.

Nothing is impossible for God. He has the power to heal sick people and save people from getting hurt. He can work miracles which we can see every single day.

So when you are one with God, when you truly trust in Him and make him a part of you and a part of your life, there is nothing you can't do!

You and He can work as one, and together, you can do amazing things.

Reflections

1. Do you think mankind could have done all the amazing things it has without the help of God?

   ....

   ....

   ....

2. Is there anything you feel that you can't do?

   ....

   ....

   ....

3. Why do you think you can't do it?

   ....

   ....

   ....

4. Think hard about what's holding you back. Tell yourself, "With God, I can do it!" and really mean it!

   ....

   ....

   ....

   ....

   ....

This week, don't let yourself believe anything is impossible. When you come across a challenge, remind yourself that with God, all things are possible.

Find Strength in Weakness

"That is why, for Christ's sake, I delight in weaknesses, in insults, in hardships, in persecutions, in difficulties. For when I am weak, then I am strong."

2 Corinthians 12:10

Weaknesses are things that we are not so good at. We usually try to hide our weaknesses from others, or pretend they don't exist.

But when God made you, He chose to create you as you are – strengths *and* weaknesses! And everything He does is for a reason.

You are amazing, smart, kind, and mature. Everything about you makes you special, and you should embrace even the things you don't always celebrate, because things that are hard make you strong.

When you overcome a challenge like a difficult subject at school or making friends in a new place, the experience makes you stronger and more capable.

Never be ashamed of your weaknesses – they are part of what makes you you!

Reflections

1. Think of some examples of weaknesses or hardships you've experienced.

2. How did you feel then?

3. Looking back, did these experiences make you strong?

4. How?

5. What is God's part in making you strong?

This week, focus on things that make you stronger. When something is hard, try to imagine how you will end up stronger for it.

PATIENCE

*"The end of something is better than its beginning.
Patience is better than pride."*

Ecclesiastes 7:8

I'm sure you've heard your parents or teachers tell you to "be patient" or to "have patience." Sometimes, it's very hard to wait for things that we want.

When we feel excited and know something good is going to happen, we can find it hard to wait our turn. But have you ever wanted something so much and then it ended too soon?

Behaving with patience means waiting calmly and trustfully for good things to come.

It means letting your friend or sibling have a turn on that new game you've been playing, even if you think you haven't played enough.

It means raising your hand and waiting patiently to be called on when you want to ask a question.

"Patience is better than pride," the Bible says. What it means is that when you are impatient or take things that are not yours to have, you think you are more important than other people.

But you know, deep down, that being prideful is wrong. So always remember – practicing patience makes you a better, more mature, and considerate girl.

Reflections

1. What does it mean to be patient?

2. Think of a time when you were patient.

3. Think of a time when you were impatient.

4. Which time turned out better, and why?

5. Why is "patience better than pride"?

This week, practice patience. Think before you speak, and don't rush things when you should take your time with them.

PRAISE

"The Lord is my strength and my shield;
my heart trusts in Him, and He helps me.
My heart leaps for joy, and with my song I praise Him."

Psalms 28:7

The book of Psalms is a collection of beautiful songs praising God and telling how wonderful He is.

Why is it so important to devote a whole book to the praise of God?

Praise is something that makes us feel good. When a teacher praises you in front of the classroom, or your coach praises you in front of the team, it shows that they appreciate you and are thankful for you.

That is what happens when we praise God, as well.

When you shout out for all the world to hear how great and incredible God's power is, and how merciful and good He is, you are expressing your gratitude and admiration for everything He does for you.

When you talk to your friends and family about your faith, and when you go to Church and praise His name, you are making the world a better place!

Reflections

1. Do you enjoy being praised?

2. Why must we praise the Lord?

3. What is your favorite hymn in the Lord's praise?

4. How can you praise the Lord in your life, outside of Church?

This week, speak in praise of God. Tell your friends and family how great He is.

SAFETY

"The name of the Lord is a fortified tower;
the righteous run to it and are safe."

Proverbs 18:10

When you are worried or afraid, you look for safety.

A tall tower with strong walls will keep you safe from everything outside – no one can get in or hurt you.

In the same way, the Lord's name is a strong tower, keeping you from harm.

When you run to Jesus to keep you safe, you can be sure that whatever it is that you were afraid of cannot touch you – because He is your protector. He promises to save and protect you always, because you are his righteous, faithful girl.

Reflections

1. Where do you feel most safe?

2. Why does that place make you feel safe?

3. To who does God provide safety?
   Can everyone shelter in the safety of His arms?

4. How can God help you feel safe?

5. What does He keep you safe from?

This week, think about how your righteousness and good deeds can keep you safe.

God is Eternal

*"The steadfast love of the Lord never ceases;
His mercies never come to an end; they are new
every morning; great is your faithfulness."*

Lamentations 3:22-23

Our kind and loving God has been here since the beginning of time, and will be here until the end of time.

Unlike Him, we are mortals – and there are some days when we are impatient, angry, or just tired. But God's patience with us, His love for us, and His mercy, never end.

That is why no matter what you do, you can always find your way back to Him. He will never stop loving you or forgiving you, just like He will always love all His children.

He is like your mom or dad – He will love you always, no matter what you do. But the greater your faith is, the more you will get from your amazing connection with Him.

So give thanks every day to the merciful Lord who will always be there for you!

Reflections

1. Do you think that God has always been and will always be?

2. What do you think there was before there was life on Earth?

3. Do you feel the Lord's love every morning?

4. If not, what can you do to make yourself feel it?

5. Which mercies does God give you?

This week, wake up every morning and reflect on how the love of the Lord manifests in your life.

Week 44

TIMING

"There's a season for everything and a time for every matter under the heavens."

Ecclesiastes 3:1

In life, we always have things to look forward to.

There's always a game you want to go to, a movie you want to see, a friend you want to hang out with, or a new accessory you want to buy.

Sometimes, things don't always work out like we want and we can't control all that happens.

Say you were really looking forward to going to the mall on Saturday to buy a new pair of earrings, but at the last minute your mom says she can't take you today because she has to watch your sibling.

Instead of being disappointed, remember that, like the Bible says, "there's a time for every matter."

God has a plan for you, and He makes time for everything you need. Believe that He has your best interests at heart and the plans He makes for you are so much better than any you could make for yourself.

Reflections

1. Do you think that everything has a right time and place?

2. Has something ever happened to you at the wrong time? How did it feel?

3. Do you have the patience to wait for things to arrive?

4. Do you ever feel that your schedule is too busy?

5. How can you stop yourself from feeling swamped?

This week, work on managing your time and schedule carefully and efficiently so that you get everything done without being overwhelmed.

Not Knowing

"For now we see only a reflection as in a mirror; then we shall see face to face. Now I know in part; then I shall know fully, even as I am fully known."

1 Corinthians 13:12

No matter how much we might want to, we can never know everything. Lots of things are unknown to us, but when we trust in the Lord, things become clearer.

When you neglect your relationship with God, you can sometimes feel lost in the darkness. You don't know where to turn to or what will happen next.

But He is always there!

He is just waiting for you to turn back and find Him, and to see clearly once again.

Reflections

1. Have you ever seen God face to face?

2. How did it feel?

3. How does it make you feel when you don't know what the future has in store?

4. What is the advantage of only knowing some things, and not knowing everything?

This week, be okay with not knowing everything. Find peace in the knowledge that God has a plan for you, even if you can't see it yet yourself.

INNER LIGHT

"You are the light of the world."

Matthew 5:14

Deep down in your soul, there is a light. Your own special inner light can shine bright and light up the world, making it a better, more wonderful place.

The light inside of you grows stronger when you are closer to God. When you pray to Him, talk to Him, and make Him a part of your life, the flame burns brighter and brighter.

As a Christian who understands and acknowledges the greatness of God, you have a responsibility to help guide others onto His path, sharing your light with them.

Your beautiful inner light is not meant to be hidden away in the darkness. You can share your light by being good and charitable, by praising the Lord and following in the ways of Christ.

Reflections

1. Do you think that everyone has a little light inside of them?

2. How does your inner light show?

3. When does it shine the brightest?

4. How can you be a light to the whole world?

This week, try to focus on other people's inner light. What makes them special?

FAITHFULNESS

*"Truly I tell you, if you have faith as small as
a mustard seed, you can say to this mountain,
'Move from here to there,' and it will move.
Nothing will be impossible for you."*

Matthew 17:20

You can have faith in all sorts of different things in your life. You can have faith in your family, in your community, in your teachers, and in yourself.

And, of course, you can have faith in God.

Having faith in something or someone means believing in them with all your heart, and trusting that you are in good hands.

When you have faith in your parents, you trust that they will raise you and care for you.

When you have faith in your teachers, you believe that they will give you a good education that will help you grow up into a knowledgeable, independent person.

And when you have complete and unwavering faith in God, it means that you understand that God is there, that He will give you strength, and that your life is in His good and kind hands.

Reflections

1. Who is the most faithful person you know?

2. When do you feel that your faith is strongest?

3. Telling a mountain to move is a metaphor for all the incredible things we can achieve. What kinds of mountains are you able to move when you have true faith in God?

This week, focus on your unwavering faith. Think of all the things your faith in the Lord could help you to achieve.

HARD WORK

*"Whatever you do, work at it with all your heart,
as working for the Lord, not for human masters,
since you know that you will receive an inheritance
from the Lord as a reward."*

Colossians 3:23-24

The very best people are those who put their heart and soul into everything they do.

As a Christian, you shouldn't be afraid of working hard and putting effort into things that are important – things like your schoolwork, helping out at home, doing charity work, and going to Church. You'll soon see just how much you grow!

When you work hard in school, you are improving your education and making yourself smarter and more knowledgeable. When you work hard helping out around the house, you are learning to be responsible and taking a load off your parents' shoulders. And when you work hard on your faith, you will be rewarded by an incredible connection with God that will last you all your life!

Reflections

1. What is your least favorite subject at school?

2. Is it hard for you to do the work required for that subject?

3. Do you sometimes find it hard to do the Lord's work? Like going to Church on Sundays or saying your daily prayers?

4. What "inheritance" can we receive from the Lord as a reward for our hard work?

This week, when you do homework or chores, think of your work as work you are doing for God, not for anyone else.

SACRIFICE

*"Greater love has no one than this:
to lay down one's life for one's friends."*

John 15:13

Sacrifice is one of the most admirable virtues in Christianity. Christ himself made the ultimate sacrifice when he chose to die for all of our sins, saving us.

You can make sacrifices in your life, too – they may be smaller, but they are still very important.

Sacrificing means being willing to give up something to help someone else. So when your mom asks you to watch over your younger siblings even though you wanted to go meet with friends, that is a sacrifice. Or when you choose to help your friend with their classwork instead of going to recess, that's a sacrifice, too.

Think about what other people sacrifice for you – like your parents, teachers, and friends.

When everyone thinks a little less about themselves and a little more about other people, the world becomes a much better place!

Reflections

1. When has someone sacrificed something for you?

2. When have you sacrificed something for someone else?

3. How did it make you feel?

4. What do we sacrifice for our relationship with God?

This week, reflect on the sacrifices people in your life make for you. Think about your parents', siblings', family's, teachers', and friends' sacrifices for you.

FEAR

"When I am afraid, I put my trust in You."

Psalms 56:3

Everyone is afraid of something.

Some people are afraid of spiders or bugs, others are afraid of heights, and some people are afraid of the dark or of being in closed spaces alone.

What are you afraid of?

You might also be afraid of bigger things – like failing a test or missing a friend who's moving far away.

When you let fear overcome you, that's all you can think about. Fear can stop you from being happy and productive and doing the things you want to do.

God tells you to "put your trust in Him" when you are afraid.

But how can putting your trust in God help you when you're scared?

Well, when you put your faith in God and trust Him with all your heart, you will realize that there's nothing to be afraid of. He is with you, holding your hand, and making sure that nothing will hurt you.

Reflections

1. What makes you afraid?

2. Who do you put your trust in when you are scared?

3. Why is it important to put our trust in the Lord?

4. What do we get from God in return when we give Him our trust?

This week, whenever you feel nervous or afraid, take deep breaths and focus on putting your full trust in the Lord.

CHALLENGES

"When you pass through the waters, I will be with you;
and when you pass through the rivers,
they will not sweep over you.
When you walk through the fire, you will
not be burned; the flames will not set you ablaze."

Isaiah 43:2

Every day, we face challenges – small and big.

A challenge can be anything from stubbing your toe on the corner of the bed to failing a test you studied hard for, or being the victim of a bully.

Even when you feel that you are alone in the face of a challenge, know that that is never true. When you put your faith in Christ, He is with you to take you over rivers and through fires and make you stronger.

The people you have in your life were put there by God so that they can do His work and help you through challenging times. So lean on them, and on your faith in God, whenever you feel the need!

Reflections

1. What challenges do you face every day?

2. What is the biggest challenge you are facing at the moment?

3. How can your faith help you to overcome these challenges?

4. How can you feel God "with you" in hard times?

This week, challenge yourself to do something hard. Focus on God's presence and how He aids you in your difficulty.

REWARD

*"Whoever pursues righteousness and love finds life,
prosperity, and honor."*

Proverbs 21:21

All year, we've talked about virtues and their reward.

We learned that if you are kind, courageous, compassionate, patient, and work hard, God will reward you with good things.

In Proverbs, we learn that the true reward for leading a life of faith and "pursuing righteousness and love" is made up of three things:

Life – a good, happy, fulfilling life.

Prosperity – success in everything that you choose to take on.

Honor – the respect and love of the people around you.

With these things in mind, keep choosing light day by day, and continue to walk God's path of grace and faith. Heavenly Father promises those who love Him and do His work on Earth that He will repay them in kind.

Reflections

1. What does it mean to be righteous?

2. How can we "pursue righteousness"?

3. In what ways can we be rewarded for doing good?

4. Write about a time when you pursued righteousness and were rewarded in return.

This week, do your best to do good by everyone around you. Look out for the good that you receive in return.

Thank you so much for reading 5-Minute Devotions for Girls!

It means the world to us to be able to bring girls just like you everywhere closer to their faith.

I hope you enjoyed your journey and feel enlightened and blessed.

We'd appreciate it so much if you would consider going to Amazon and leaving a review.

Your reviews help us bring you more beautiful and meaningful content like this book.

About Made Easy Press

At Made Easy Press, our goal is to bring you beautifully designed, thoughtful gifts and products.

We strive to make complicated things – easy. Whether it's learning new skills or putting memories into words, our books are led by values of family, creativity, and self-care and we take joy in creating authentic experiences that make people truly happy.

Look out for other books by Made Easy Press here!

Made in the USA
Las Vegas, NV
19 December 2023

83260379R00066